WHAT DO I DO WITH THIS?

1 minimalist minute

CLAUDIA DAVIDE MONTALTO

WHAT DO I DO WITH THIS?

1 minimalist minute

The quick decision-making method to get time in your life, space in your home and save money forever

Second edition: April 2022

Author: © Claudia Davide Montalto

Cover design: © Gonzalo Herce (Inkoherente)

Photography: © Eloi Herrero Calvo

Translator: © Júlia Silva

ISBN: 979-84-53637-90-4

This book is dedicated to my daughter.

I also dedicate it to all the people

who desire a more serene, free and pleasant life.

One minute of success is worth years of failure.

Robert Browning (1812-1889)

Every inch of space is a miracle.

Walt Whitman (1819-1892)

Money does not certainly bring joy; but it isn't an obstacle to it either.

Josep Pla (1897-1981)

Contents

Smart Book

This book will offer you a unique experience that goes beyond the next few pages. I am going to provide you with exclusive multimedia content. You can ask me any questions you want and I will answer them with pleasure.

To start with, you can access a playlist created by me, with songs specially selected to accompany you while reading this book. I'm sure you will like them!

https://open.spotify.com/playlist/5FmEDvLcZNHUe6vVs3t XU3?si=4b7d12f7f8ee47ab

Questions, suggestions, curiosities?

https://linktr.ee/claudia.davide.montalto

Introduction

With varying intensity, we all want more freedom, more time, more space and more money. However, we almost never know where to start to achieve what we aspire to. Sometimes we decide to follow and receive guidance from some "infallible guide" only to realise that it doesn't work for us or we are faced with a thousand obstacles. Every person is unique, everybody's life is unmatched and therefore it is impossible to find a strict one-size fits all formula. It is imperative that we begin to take control of our lives, develop intuition and accept that we are unique and hence must draw on our personal experiences for self-development.

This modest book will teach you a very simple and quick method that will allow you to decide in 1 minute (or less!) what you need, and I dare say, the following pages will add value to your life. My aim for this book is to help you achieve a perfect awareness of what serves you and what doesn't; that you may also become conscious that you should not have around you what doesn't serve you. At the end of the book you will see how you can improve emotionally and economically, without becoming a minimalist.

For years I lived with a feeling of suffocation in my own home. No matter how many things I had, it always seemed that it still wasn't enough. I felt a permanent dissatisfaction, I wanted more and more things. Everything had a potential desire for appropriation, which made me believe that if I wanted something and I acquired it, then I'd be a little happier. Nothing could be further from the truth.

Over time and due to different circumstances of my life, I was forced to experiment with detachment from material things. What seemed so complicated and painful, turned out to be one of the best existential achievements of my life and turned out to be the precise opposite of a minimalist life.

Consciously or not, in our daily lives we seek all kinds of freedoms, however, the ones that stand out always have the same basis: less responsibilities, less worries, less negative feelings and greater financial freedom. We want a good, peaceful and comfortable life, but we spend our time submerged in its opposites, suffocating among material possessions and complaining about insufficient time and money for other purposes.

Once we experience the freedom of not having so much, our world changes significantly. The most difficult thing is precisely identifying what that "so much" is, the norm being that everything seems "not enough" to us whereas money is never "so much"! With the method I've named "1 Minute Minimalist", you can quickly find the answer to what "so much" is! I wish I could have defined it years ago...

I confess that my philosophy of life has a Minimalist inclination, but not in the sense we are used to seeing, hearing or feeling. So before you read on, I want to make the following clear:

▪ This book does not present Minimalism as the foolproof fix for all problems or the panacea for every hardship in life.

▪ It does not teach how to clean and keep your home.

- It won't tell you how to fold your clothes and organise your wardrobe in a gradient of colours.

- It won't instruct you to throw everything out the window for you to find everlasting happiness.

- It won't overly advocate the theory of a sustainable world.

- It does not present the conformism associated with scarcity or deprivation of goods.

- It does not assume a transformative power when applied to all areas of humanity.

- It does not negate beauty when it doesn't serve a purpose.

- It does not induce anti-consumerism or denote consumerism as the devil on earth.

- And, obviously, it is not a maximalist book.

This one book, in its modest simplicity and minimal presentation, will change your perspective on the most basic things in life and you'll find that it is not so difficult to fulfil your desires if you know how to adapt the Minimalist style to your character and your surroundings. With a detailed and at the same time general approach, we simply use Minimalism to illuminate the life and economy of each one.

It's been proven to the highest personal standards, and you can prove it now too!

1. Personal background

I was born on the outskirts of Lisbon, Portugal, in 1977. In my early years, there wasn't much time in my home, nor space or money; but I was a lucky child and I followed a path that, even if slowly, enabled me to evolve positively regarding these three pillars of well-being.

When I was young I didn't have many things and I didn't give too much importance to what I had. Even though I had few toys, my room was the biggest mess I knew of. None of my friends had as many things out of place as I did. Sometimes I had to jump between pieces and bits of whatever was completely covering the floor.

I suppose my parents had no time to be angry with me and were content if the chaos didn't extend beyond the walls of my room. But when everything was put away in storage boxes and the best cared for toys returned to the shelf, a sense of peace and serenity fell over me and every corner of my existence. I will never forget those extraordinary emotions. I loved having more free space, walking without stumbling and feeling the purest air inside my house!

At the age of 18, I began a stage of successive changes of residence. The reasons that led to so many changes were various; either to study a subject that appealed to me, to have a better job, a higher salary, or because I didn't feel comfortable where I lived. I was always looking for existential perfection, the one that would transform me into a "pain-free" happy person. Yes, I was convinced that, in that way, I would be able to achieve my much-desired happiness. Not that I was unhappy, but I felt that I still lacked more, although I could not define what this "more", that I should achieve or attain, was. Luckily, all these changes were always voluntary and conscious.

First I moved to Évora, 120 kms away from my parents and sister, to study. I graduated in Philosophy. Then I moved back to Lisbon to study Human Resources Management. Next move, this time to Barcelona (Spain), was to advance my professional career in the area of Labour Law and Administration in different multinational companies. Then I moved to Sevilla and later to Toulouse (France). Since 2011, I have been living in Barcelona with my partner, my daughter and 2 dogs. I have finally settled down! I work as a Consultant, but, although I have various professional recognitions, I am not satisfied with them and I find in writing the possibility to share my experiences or knowledge to help and inspire other people.

I carried out each of the relocations almost always in the same way, taking with me only one big suitcase. Everything that mattered to me fit in that suitcase. You could say I was travelling and moving light.

I would settle in the new house and, although I sometimes missed some useful objects, I was very happy just for the fact of starting a "new life". However, the reality, on the whole was not like that. I suffered fear and anxiety for being in an unknown place, surrounded by unknown people and all the uncertainty that such challenges implied. The joy, excitement and tranquillity I enjoyed in the early days of each move were, after all, because of the little material possessions I had, although, I must confess, that in those days I wasn't aware of it. I shared my personal space with few things. Organising and cleaning was very easy and I didn't waste time with insignificant things. The essentials were there and I didn't need more.

At that time I didn't have to work hard and I had more energy than ever to dedicate myself to what interested me and gave me pleasure. I didn't spend money on things I didn't need, because I might not have liked the new place and would soon move again. In that case, the less things I had, the easier it would be to leave the new residence to start again in a different one. At best, I would buy some decorative elements to embellish and personalise my space. I had a tendency for Minimalism and I didn't know it! I was not able to identify the attraction for the simple, for the less, for the light and practical.

Now I understand that it isn't moving that determines that desired tranquility, but how we intentionally create the characteristics of our home, our life and our economy.

Regrettably and proportionally to the passing of time, my house began to fill up and became like so many others. After a few months, I would lose that feeling of having infinite oxygen and control over things. I would go back to spending money on whims that never satisfied my true desires, an attempt to make them an escape from the occasional loneliness, and a snowball would roll down the mountain of well-being, becoming an avalanche that swept the rest away. The thing is, by buying things to fill not physical but emotional voids, we enter an infinite spiral, and the more we want to free ourselves from a heavy and limited life, the more we consume, the more we spend and the more we regret it, only to then try to undo our mistakes and correct them the same way. We already know that this system doesn't work, and through the 20-plus houses I have lived in, the 20-plus changes of neighbourhoods, cities or countries, I have realised that a solution was feasible.

2. The two faces of Minimalism

Minimalism as an artistic current emerged around the year 1960, when the world was beginning to recover from the destructive and chaotic effects of the Second World War. As the term itself indicates, it is characterised by minimising the activity of the artist in favour of an increase in the action of the spectator. In our lives we are both artists and spectators, so it is of paramount importance to balance the relationship between the two. We must be fully aware that extremes are never beneficial, as well as to know how to adapt to ourselves the best that this movement has to offer.

At first, Minimalism was an architectural movement, but its increasing recognition made it so popular that it expanded to other arts such as painting, sculpture, music and design. Nowadays, the notoriety of Minimalist art allows its application to as many aspects of life as we want and there are numerous features that we can attribute to it: simplicity, dematerialization, harmony, luminosity, purity, lessening, sitting on simple forms, neutral or soft colours, among many others.

Minimalism is characterised by a vocabulary that often contradicts itself. If we speak of simplicity and lessening, aren't we indicating emptiness and scarcity? If we talk about dematerialization, aren't we showing limitation and conformism?

Let us see some practical examples: my house has a Minimalist style, it is simple, with white walls, only one painting hanging in one of the spaces, a few unsophisticated decorative ornaments and some souvenirs while everything else is of constant use. I often dress in comfortable clothes, with basic designs of plain fabrics or discreet prints, neutral colours and of fairly moderate monetary value. Can this be defined as mediocrity and insipidity? No, but if we take the Minimalist culture to the extreme, we run the risk of falling into Ultra-Minimalism which I don't consider to be the right path to a fair and fulfilling life. The sensible thing is to take from this movement what suits us best, what we consider provides us space and time, liberation from what we identify as superfluous, capacity for amplitude and vision on what builds our happiness when considered the ultimate life goal.

If, per chance, Ultra-Minimalism is our motto, then we should renounce all kinds of non-essential material possessions. In this case, we should be content with having only what we need for our basic needs, giving up any decorative elements and thus annihilating everything beyond the basic and necessary, and we would also have to have an almost cashless bank account, since we don't need much to live on.

All over social media and information and entertainment channels there are lots of profiles of people (some of them influencers) who boast of a lifestyle just as I describe and it is, almost inevitable, to feel persuaded to discard our belongings in order to achieve a similar false happiness. Their reasons for adopting such traits are the consideration that Minimalism is the irrefutable and natural answer to achieving a perfect existence, just as other disciplines, lifestyles or religions. The Minimalist lifestyle taken to the extreme considers that everything is a hindrance and the less we possess, the better. I fear that the extreme Minimalist philosophy has become another trend of the 21st century, however, it is likely that it is nothing more than an appearance far removed from reality and authenticity of those who preach it.

Each person's personal identity remains essential, and it is impossible to maintain it consistently when trying to survive on its facade alone. We must go deeper, explore the value that this trend can offer us and extract its benefits. It's no use investing in a route if we don't take advantage of its best paths and landscapes. And let's not forget our goal: I am the number one priority, not what I have, what I have had or what I will have in the future. We should avoid consumerism, as an addiction, without giving up controlled and favourable consumption for our own existence and for the hoped-for growth, without fearing a possible deprivation because this will make our objective go down the drain.

If I love reading, why can't I have hundreds of books in my house? If I am passionate about painting, why can't I cover my walls with paintings? If I love to collect watches, why can't I have as many as I want? This goes against Minimalism, of course, but this is precisely where we have to seek balance. It is necessary that you know how to filter what comes into your life, what you decide to let into your life. The choice of a minimalist style can also be arbitrary, I don't have to resign myself to all the things that are not essential. It is not necessary to scream at full lungs that I am willing to leave everything behind and go live in a cabin in the middle of the woods. We are human beings and as such complex, we cannot pretend to live in a world characterised by indestructible simplicity. Recognising this great truth will allow you to prevent the mistake of living in extremis.

On the other hand, Minimalism is also a source of pleasure, because the detachment from the material generates a sensation of profound liberation, compared to a backpack of stones that we carry on our shoulders and then take off, leaving it on the ground. Similar to when we have a need that is satisfied, ceasing to exist, and the pleasure that arises as an immediate effect.

Plenitude is attainable when we become aware that we do not need to possess an infinitude of objects and, at the same time, are able to choose what matters and put the minimalist forces at our service to simplify life, lighten the soul and save forever.

3. Simplify Life – Time, Space, Freedom and Quality

One of the most extraordinary aspects of implementing Minimalism is the ability to provide a serene, orderly and clean environment. With fewer objects, the time required by the totality of material belongings decreases considerably. It is not the same to have 20 shirts than to have 7. It is not the same to accumulate 15 bottles of cosmetics in the bathroom than to have only 4. I am not only talking about the space they occupy, but also about all the necessary maintenance and their real usefulness.

Out of 20 shirts, I have 6 or 7 I prefer and those are precisely the ones that make me feel better, I have no reason to wear the others. Consequently, I should not keep them in my wardrobe. There will be someone who will wear them more than me. And what does it matter if people always see me wearing the same ones?

When we realise what is substantial and important, it is very easy to renounce to what is only meant to be ostentatious. Once again, I am not what I have (nor the clothes I wear!) and it is much more valuable to be comfortable than to rely on appearances, even if I repeat outfits. It's not about wearing the same clothes every day, but the same or similar clothes, having a limited but sufficient quantity. In fact, more and more successful personalities are giving us their example: take Steve Jobs and Barack Obama for instance. It is a choice that saves time when making decisions every morning; it allows us to feel good every day because we always wear something we like and it is comfortable; it saves money because there is no desire to buy a variety of pieces. In short, we save on hassle and are more free to move forward in the logical direction of life.

Out off the 15 plastic jars distributed between the sink and the bathtub, I waste an average of 7.5 seconds a day (45 minutes a year) just to identify the one I want to grab and put it back with the rest. To this we add the necessary cleaning time, around 182 minutes per year. It doesn't sound like much, but let's not forget that this is just one example of the dozens of excessive things that surround us.

By eliminating the superfluous, we have more time to focus on what we consider important and valuable. Whatever that might be: social relationships, hobbies, work, entertainment, knowledge, experiences... Reducing the superfluous will give way to a less fragmented attention span, the elimination of worthless items from our to-do list, greater mental flexibility and better emotional management.

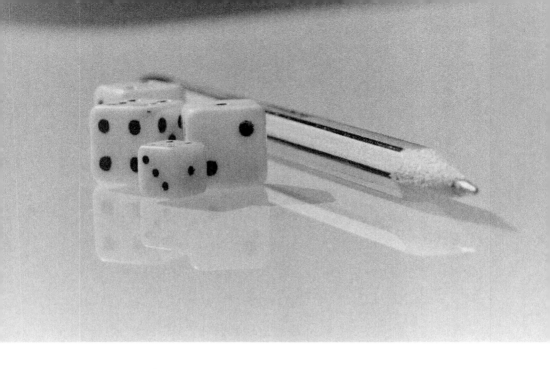

Never forget that your home is the most important place in the world! It is where you can experience your greatest joys and sorrows despite social values, where you feel safe and secure. So, it's best to tailor it to your inner peace, comfort and general well-being.

Now imagine two different types of houses with opposite characteristics: one is serene, orderly, clean, decorated in soft colours and simple lines, both in furnishings and in all the accessories. The other is the opposite: strong colours, excessive furniture loaded with objects and with so little space to move around that we immediately realise how difficult it is to find anything in the midst of so many things.

These two types of homes undoubtedly lead us to two types of feelings: the first provides calm, tranquillity, serenity, control, relaxation and well-being. The second indicates confusion, anxiety, imprisonment, dispersion and discomfort, right? So, isn't it incredibly wonderful that you can choose a part of your emotions? As much as the world might be sometimes cruel, it's amazing that our most private space doesn't become an additional constraint on our happiness. There are things that interfere with our feelings and emotions, so we have to know how to choose them carefully. These same things alter our free time, our space, our freedom and our quality of life.

A house free of burdens is a luminous place. An exuberant clarity that almost allows us to feel harmony at our fingertips. It is genuine elegance.

4. Saving and Earning – Money matters

If I am on a Minimalist path, won't saving money and having high capitalist power go against the very meaning of Minimalism? Never.

If I get rid of useless things and do not waste money on what serves no purpose, and, as I mentioned before, I am saving time for more interesting matters, these same matters are the key to my well-being and allow me to enjoy a splendid life. It turns out that precisely the interesting matters almost always need a monetary impulse. If my dream is to visit Antarctica, I could have done with not wasting monstrous amounts of money on objects that in 90% of the cases bring nothing of value to my life and the fulfilment of my dream.

The calculations are simple: let's imagine that every month we buy things that we don't really need, spending 40€. In most cases, the unnecessary spending is far more than 40 euros per month, but let's use this amount as an example. If you had known in advance of the uselessness and had avoided the purchase, in just 12 months you would have saved 480€. How many savings accounts, pension plans, indexed investments or financial funds give you so much in a single year without investing or fronting up a single euro? I think the answer is logical, you can be your source of income without almost realising it!

It is crucial to keep spending to a smart level in order to be able to apply it to what fills our soul and vitalizes our body. By this doesn't mean you can't save to buy something material. Of course you can! If you want a state-of-the-art mobile phone and consider it to be an asset in your life, then you will carry out your goals accordingly, but without ever losing track and keeping your Minimalist philosophy in mind. Otherwise, success is not guaranteed.

Besides all the money we can save by avoiding excesses that serve no purpose, there is another important aspect related to money within this context supported by Minimalism, which I shall express next.

From the hundreds of things that we have in our house, many of them can be sold to generate extra money. From the most basic and useless things, such as pieces of clothing from our children when they were young, to things of greater value, such as home appliances or electronic devices, can be sold. It's a win-win situation for both the one selling and the buyer. I'm sure there are plenty of people who wish they had what you no longer want, but don't have the purchasing power for a new, so by

simply taking a photo and uploading it to Wallapop or any other type of Marketplace, app or other platforms, potential buyers will contact you in order to reach a deal and make business easily. In fact, platforms for selling second-hand items are growing fast and more and more users are looking for an object-money exchange. In any way is the purchase of second-hand goods considered inelegant or even tacky, quite the contrary: the reutilisation of material goods takes on special importance in a world that we want to be increasingly sustainable.

Even things that are broken and no longer work can be sold. Two months ago, I sold a dishwasher that wouldn't start. A very nice man, who recycles parts from old appliances, came to my house to pick it up and paid me 50 euros. It would have been easier to have it collected when the new one was brought in, however, it took me 5 minutes to post the ad and arrange the day and time with the gentleman. We were both pleased with the transaction.

As I am deciding what I want to keep and what not, I am also moving along the correct path of deciding what I do or do not want to acquire. I no longer welcome something into my home without thinking about it. Every time you are on the street or on a shopping site and the opportunity to spend money presents itself to you, in an almost automatic way, you will analyse the advantages and disadvantages of the acquisition before acting. You will see how magnificent the result is!

Remember that buying more does not make you happier. It is a physiological matter of dopamine increase, translated into an ephemeral pleasure, with which we unsuccessfully heal emotional injuries. Mindless buying is the same as trying to give ourselves a reward for having failed in other areas, or to replace unachieved pleasure in other existential aspects.

In the next chapter, we come to the most important part of this book, how we can overcome the difficulty of choosing what stays and what goes.

5. The Method – Minimalist Action

The method I present is, in itself, Minimalist. It leads to immediate action as a result of a conscious, logical, simple and clear decision. We aim to identify what should be part of our environment and what not, as well as to avoid approaching elements that contribute nothing to us. I took the liberty of naming it "1 Minimalist Minute" because of its simplicity and rapid results.

The main pillar of this minimalist minute consists in considering all material beings and simply dividing them into two groups: Positive Objects and Negative Objects.

Positive Objects are, as the very semantic indicates, endowed with positivity, that is, their typology defines them as contributors to our well-being. They may be positive due to a certain isolated and unique characteristic, or simultaneous characteristics. Positive Objects are the set that matter most to us and affect us most, since most of the time they have a permanent and visible presence in our lives, although on many occasions in an unconscious way.

Negative Objects are, of course, the opposite, but only to a certain extent. They don't contribute anything at all to our lives, they don't make our daily lives easier or more joyful, and not even their presence is pleasant, so we usually keep them out of our field of vision. We tend to push Negative Objects away from out of field of vision because we can't even acknowledge their harmful impact.

We do not separate ourselves from them *ad eternun* because of their false utilitarian potential, which we keep alive, deferring day after day their possible and hidden positivity. This type of object ends up harming the virtue of Positive Objects, which is why it is recommended to avoid them and never seek to replace them with similar ones.

Apparently, it is neither an easy nor pleasant task to decide whether an object is Positive or Negative and, consequently, to act in accordance with the decision.

Nonetheless, this method explains in 3 steps how we can take equitable and efficient decisions to build our Minimalist world and make an intelligent money management.

Let's have a look at the method stages, which are built upon 3 concepts related to the characteristics of all material things:

1 - Utility

2 - Aesthetic

3 - Affection

We should always follow them in an orderly way if we intend to reach the satisfaction offered by Minimalism "adapted" to each individual being. None of the concepts is susceptible of being eliminated from the methodical chain, but the 3 can be simultaneously implicit in the same object and, in this case, lead us to conclude that the object is, without a shadow of doubt, a Positive Object.

For a better understanding, let's take a closer look at each one of them:

The **Utility** of an object refers to its real benefit as a facilitator of an activity, whether by necessity or whim, but always a proven utility. The verification is made as follows: the object must have been used at least once in the last 12 months or, if I don't have it yet and I am considering acquiring it, I must be sure that I will use it immediately. Otherwise, we cannot attribute the quality of usefulness to a material good, as this would be to mislead our conscience which will result in the disadvantages being greater than the benefits. There are things that we use every day, others every week and others only sporadically. We can't give to an occasion, which is often conditioned to a certain time of the year, a power greater than it deserves. We should not allow the occasional usefulness of an object to occupy a permanent space in our lives with all that this implies, and even more so when this usefulness is not only a possibility, and in most cases it is not even effective.

Something that is used less than once a year can be replaced by an alternative strategy, for example, if I keep some skis in my house because every winter I enjoy a weekend skiing in the Alps, it is preferable to get rid of them, recover part of the investment by selling them second-hand and then, if I want to ski at Christmas, I can rent all the equipment for the 3 or 4 days I need. I free up space, recuperate money and don't spend time with its maintenance. There is, therefore, a personal impartiality and a clear objectivity. In short, skis are in principle a Negative Object. Nevertheless, they still contain within themselves the possibility of being considered a Positive Object until I finish the method of analysis that will lead me to the final decision of whether to keep them or not.

Aesthetics appears as the second step after inquiring about the usefulness of an object. If in the previous phase we concluded that the object is useless or unnecessary, we will now submit it to an aesthetic study. I don't need the skis, but they are the "apple of my eye", I love to watch them and even have them hanging on a wall as if they were a piece of art. I enjoy their presence, the representation of beauty and the enigmatic attraction they have. They make me feel good when I observe them or just by the fact of feeling their presence in my home, they bring beauty to my days.

We know that there is no rational basis behind what perception defines as beauty and here again, Minimalism is debatable. However, this does not mean that one cannot evaluate the material world in its entirety under the light of Aesthetics in a broad sense and use it to our advantage, adapt it to our values and desires, shaping the Minimalist philosophy as it suits us best and from there reap its best fruits.

It is convenient to remember that Aesthetics has nothing to do with the monetary value of an object. Without knowing the price attributed by someone to an article, we can distinguish and elaborate our criteria on whether it is beautiful or ugly, pleasant, or unpleasant.

In this case we can no longer speak of an impartiality connected to the analysis carried out in the previous phase, because beauty does not imply a rational and empirical judgement. In its simplicity, it is or is not. Between what we consider beautiful or ugly, we feel unease or well-being, pleasure or displeasure towards the object and that is a subjective argument. Still, aesthetic evaluation does not lose its importance in the decision-making method because each of us is unique and we perceive the world in different ways, with all its peculiarities.

It is you who decides to consider an Object Positive or Negative in the Aesthetic phase of the method, just as in the first and third phases. It may happen that in this analysis you find yourself doubting, which is normal, it may happen that you like an object, but not too much, and then you don't know what to do with it. This is why it is important whether it is visible in your home or not. If it is stored in some cupboard and you keep it, it will continue to occupy space without there being a logical reason for it. If you get rid of that "pretty-ish" object you run the risk of regretting it. In any case, I can guarantee that 99% of the things we decide to discard, once out of our private and intimate world, we will never remember them again.

Affection is what impacts most on our feelings in general and our emotional state of mind in particular. It is the last of the 3 steps in the decision making process and the most complex.

It may seem very complicated to say "no" to something you have always said "yes" to. We open our treasure chest of memories, and all its contents are important, all the objects represent people or emotions to which we have attached affection at some point in our life and this makes a decision change difficult. We should identify and select what is really important. It is likely that if we don't make an objective observation, everything will be important, and we won't be able to see the choice that perhaps we are overvaluing. In this sense, we must make room for moderation and not allow too many memories in physical format. Things that, every 5 years, we look at, touch and smile at are not worth it. We would have to ask ourselves: if I didn't have those things, would I stop smiling when they emerge in my consciousness?

Let's put the scenario in a more radical perspective: When life comes to an end, how will we take those memories with us? In a suitcase? Of course not, what represents affection in physical form will never be eternal and like all other things, will not pass into the spiritual dimension, if that is what we want to call it.

The intention is not to eliminate all memories, no, that would be impossible, besides, your past experiences are part of you. What you must do is select in detail the valuable memories, the memories that make your eyes shine and that fill your heart. All other memories do not need a physical representation. It is enough to have to manage it in an emotional dimension and in our mind.

If there are symbols of affection, of genuine affection, yes, keep those symbols close to you, observe them, feel them. But always be selective and free yourself from the elements of the past that are not relevant and do not even contribute to anything in the present. Choose with discernment, observing your emotion in the first 5 seconds that you look at the object and you will see how easy it is to decide. Say goodbye to what does not move you enough, to what does not alter your emotions to make you feel better.

Let us now look at the method in a general way. Thinking, deciding, and acting are the dynamic parts. And I assure you that they can be done in just one minute:

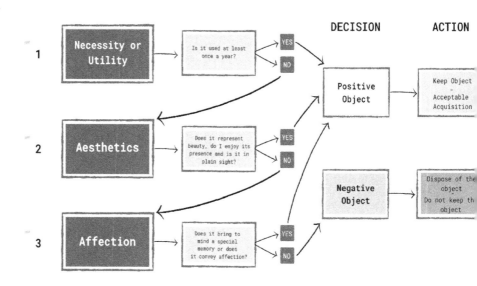

You can also find this diagram here: https://cutt.ly/UQ1ZNPN

This minimalist question-answer method is, after all, an introspection with practical and immediate results. By taking as a starting point closed questions that allow nothing more than 2 options of response ("Yes" or "No"), we are immediately led to a decision and, consequently, to action.

How long does it take us to answer 3 questions with such limited response options? 1 minute! I would even dare to say less than 1 minute, but I would also not like to see this method dubbed "pretentious", and it is not necessary to waste your breath on this prototype of choices.

In practice, let's suppose that at the bottom of a drawer we have stored our previous mobile phone, with a scratched screen. It still works, but it has been replaced by a more modern one:

First question: is this phone useful? It was, but not anymore.

Second question: is it beautiful and do I have it displayed as if it were an artistic creation or a museum piece? Also no.

Third question: Does it convey any special feeling of affection or any other positive emotion to me? My old mobile phone may remind me of all or almost all the experiences I have had in the last two years, but it is not in itself a conveyor of affection and, moreover, it contains implicit negative emotions, so there is no point in keeping it.

There, at the speed of sound, a light goes on in our consciousness, giving us a rational, objective clarity and an emotional relief. Now, we intelligently know that we have to do something with one more object. In this case, we have to remove it from our life and benefit from everything I mentioned in the two previous chapters of this book.

In the same way, the 3 questions should be present whenever we think of buying something, of bringing something new into our environment, that is, the method applies both to what you have and to what you might possibly have.

As I decide what I want to keep and what not, I will also become more conscious of my decisions regarding what I want to have.

It is essential to follow this method, wherever and whenever; this is a relevant virtue that it has, so it is not limited to a localised and temporal application, but we can follow the process at home or elsewhere whenever the opportunity to acquire something presents itself.

For example, I walk into a bazaar crammed with a plethora of objects. Let's imagine that 10% of those objects might come in handy. I look at a tablecloth and a set of cloth napkins, they are pretty and cheap... But do I really want to spend my money on them? Do I want to take up another bit of my house with it and waste time on maintaining it?

Similarly, following the methodology, an affirmative answer to just one of the 3 questions about usefulness, aesthetics or affection, is already enough to identify what I should own. Without remorse nor guilt.

You must have realised that there are many more possibilities of identifying positive objects than negative objects. That is why it is so important to apply the method and act coherently with the results, trying to give balance to your life so that you can benefit from the advantages of your logical decisions.

Going back to the practical aspect of the decision method, when the first, second or third question is answered with a "no", it is time to choose what we will do with the object to be discarded. Here we enter a phase that is less complicated, since there is a multitude of options, all of them valid, none being worse or better than the others.

We are free beings; we do what we want with what we no longer want! I can think of donating the object if it still has some characteristic that can benefit another person. However, if the object has a high monetary value, it can be sold and get a second life in with someone else. Here, as when we choose to recycle (and not sell), we are committing ourselves to a more sustainable world and this should always be an element of our daily lives.

So, to offer, recycle, sell or, in last case scenario, throw away, the choice is up to you. At least it will always be a choice according to the time and energy we have available to dispose of the objects, as well as what we consider recommendable.

Afterwards, enjoy the lightness. You will already feel it from the first decision, and you can multiply it as many times as you wish.

It is not necessary to assume that "having nothing is the best". In fact, we did not live better in prehistory nor were our ancestors better people.

Don't you think there is a connection here between having and being?

It is essential to HAVE, of course, but the important thing is to know how to HAVE with control, to HAVE what is important, whether for its usefulness, aesthetics or affection. If you master this simple 1-minute technique, I guarantee you will feel better. Personally, I do not hide my proud result of having started to follow the method many years ago. Maybe at the beginning I didn't follow it in a perfect way. The change was gradual, and time made me more assertive, achieving extraordinary results. Now I have more money in my account, more space in my house and more free time to dedicate to what I like. More than that, the freedom and lightness that I breathe every day is inexplicable in words.

6. What if I don't do it?

If after everything you've read in this book you decide to do nothing with many of the things you have or think you have, if you decide not to apply the "1 Minimalist Minute" method, you have every right to do so and you will continue to accumulate things and more things, you won't save money for what you are really passionate about or what increases your well-being and makes you happier. Nor will you have more time to enjoy your favourite activities or more space to expand your freedom.

This book, unlike many others, does not dictate a set of laws or seek to impose impersonal standards on you to achieve a "truly minimalist" life. I invite you to think for yourself, proposing that you adapt Minimalism to your existential purposes, with a simple and practical method of identifying what is important to you.

The actions suggested do not have the purpose of making you live with the minimum of material goods possible. I am sure that life is not more sublime if we have nothing or little, but it is if what we have is what brings us harmony, serenity, peace and happiness. The rest should not take up any space.

The type of Minimalism I suggest prioritises well-being, which means more time, more space, more quality, more freedom and more money. At the same time, it is a resource for self-knowledge as you go deeper into your choices.

I have written based on my experience, so I can assure you that if you decide to follow the method step by step, you will achieve the goal of living lighter, which will give you a lot of satisfaction.

The time you invest in reading this book gives you a tangible reward. Because organising your life results in well-being. In just one minute you will be able to identify what deserves to continue occupying space around you and within you, and what you should eliminate in order to have more harmony.

I introduce you to the practice of a conscious and adaptable minimalism. Without falling into extremes that, far from bringing you benefits, can affect your happiness.

My aim is that you have a better relationship with yourself and your surroundings, and that this relationship bears fruit in your mental, emotional, spiritual, and physical well-being.

Remember that Minimalism is not the goal, it does not have an end in itself, it is one more path that you can choose like many others, but more effective and faster in order to have a pleasant life, without complications. A path that helps us shape our existence, with positive qualities for each one of us and for the planet. If you know how to adapt it to your needs and desires, you end up gaining a lot.

The choice is always yours! You are the only one who knows what is best for you, don't stop, push the worthless distractions out of your way and find what is worthwhile!

Minimalist Diary – The Intensive Process

A few months ago, I set myself a personal challenge and, applying the method I have just taught you, I went into a deep cleaning process. I turned my house upside down, analysed each of my things and dug deep into my treasure chest of memories. I must confess that it was a very productive exercise and beneficial to my happiness.

Motivated by a game created by 2 minimalist authors (Joshua Fields Millburn and Ryan Nicodemus) who claim to have changed their lives thanks to Minimalism, I decided to experience the difficulties and results of such game.

The common thread of the transformation game is very simple: a 30-day process period, in which we start day 1 by getting rid of 1 object from our house; on day 2, we eliminate 2 objects, on day 3, 3 objects and so on in a successive pace until day 30, in which we must give up 30 things. In total, if everything goes well, we will get to the end of the game with 465 less objects in our house.

During this journey of intense minimalist intention, I took some notes in a personal journal mode, with a degree of intimacy enough to be shared and thus, perhaps, inspire readers to grab the reins of their lives with more strength, to follow the

"1 Minute Minimalist" method, to make decisions and translate them into actions. If you're eventually curious, you can take a look at my 30 day journal here: https://cutt.ly/YQ13kK7

Do you feel like helping out?

If you liked this book, write your review on Amazon, share what you thought and help other people to discover the benefits of the method I presented to you. It will take you 1 minute!

I'm very keen on hearing your opinion and I'm also here to give you a hand if you want to find out more or if you'd like to clarify any issue. Write me back!

https://linktr.ee/claudia.davide.montalto

Thank you!

Printed in Great Britain
by Amazon